GIRAFFE

by Caroline Arnold
Photographs by Richard Hewett

WILLIAM MORROW & COMPANY, INC. · NEW YORK

PHOTO CREDITS: Permission to use the following photographs is gratefully acknowledged: Caroline Arnold, page 22; Eliot Brenowitz, pages 12, 13; Ron Garrison, San Diego Zoo, page 11; Six Flags Great Adventure Safari Park, pages 42–3, 44.

Library of Congress Cataloging-in-Publication Data. Arnold, Caroline. Giraffe. Includes index. Summary: Describes the characteristics and habits of giraffes and discusses life for these animals at a large open-air wildlife park in New Jersey. 1. Giraffes—Juvenile literature. 2. Six Flags Great Adventure Safari Park (N.J.)— Juvenile literature. [1. Giraffes. 2. Six Flags Great Adventure Safari Park (N.J.)]
I. Hewett, Richard, ill. II. Title.
QL737.U56A76 1987 599.73′57 87-1502 ISBN 0-688-07069-8 I ISBN 0-688-07070-1 (lib. bdg.)

ACKNOWLEDGMENTS

We want to thank the Six Flags Great Adventure Safari Park in Jackson, New Jersey, for the opportunity to photograph the giraffes in this book. We are grateful to all the park personnel who cooperated with us in this project, and in particular we thank David Barnes (pictured above), Senior Supervisor of Animal Care, for his time, cheerful assistance, and expert advice. We also thank Angela Hewett and John Levin for all their help, and our editor, Andrea Curley, for her continuing enthusiasm and support.

Craning his long, spotted neck, the young giraffe peered from behind his mother's back, and with wide brown eyes he watched the approaching truck. Was the driver one of the people who worked at the park? Perhaps someone was bringing more food or coming to give him a friendly pat on the nose. Maybe it was a visitor who had come to see the animals that lived in the African plains section of the wildlife park.

The young giraffe was one of sixteen giraffes that lived at an open-air wild-life park in central New Jersey. After his birth four months earlier, the keepers had named him Easter because he had been born on Easter morning. Unlike wild giraffes, Easter and the other giraffes had become used to having people nearby. Still, Easter was always cautious and waited for the other giraffes to move first when there were people around.

Like wild giraffes, the giraffes in the park are curious about newcomers in their area and often stand in the road to greet them. Visitors to the park are instructed not to touch or feed the animals. Even though the giraffes seem quite tame, they are not pets, and they must be treated as wild animals. Giraffes are gentle, but if they become frightened or angry, they can be dangerous. Even the keepers, who know the animals very well, are careful near them.

In the wild, giraffes live in central and southern Africa on dry, grassy plains that are dotted with acacia trees, the giraffe's favorite food. Wildlife parks and zoos try to duplicate natural living conditions as much as possible. Easter and the other animals lived in large, grassy enclosures where there were food, shelter, and plenty of room to move about freely. Although the weather and vegetation in New Jersey were different from those in Africa, the park was a comfortable home and allowed the giraffes to behave much as they do in the wild.

Most of us will never have the chance to see giraffes in their real home in Africa. But by visiting zoos and wildlife parks, we can see these strange-looking creatures up close and learn more about them.

Giraffes have amazed people for a long time. Over four thousand years ago, they were imported to Egypt and put on display there. But the giraffe was such an unusual-looking animal that people did not know what to make of it. Because it had spots like a leopard, and a long neck and two-toed hooves like those of a camel, the ancient Romans called it a "camel leopard." This belief is reflected today in the giraffe's scientific name, *Giraffa camelopardalis*.

Okapi

However, the giraffe is not directly related to either camels or leopards. Rather, it is descended from long-necked animals that roamed through Europe, Asia, and Africa millions of years ago. Today, all these ancient animals are extinct.

The only close living relative of the giraffe is the okapi. The okapi, which stands about 6 feet (1.8 meters) tall, lives in the dense forests of central Africa. Its narrow stripes help it to blend into its surroundings. Like the giraffe, it has an elongated neck and short, knobby horns on its head.

Masai giraffe

All giraffes are the same species and are similar in body size, habits, and behavior. However, there are several different types, or subspecies, each with a slightly different spot pattern. The Masai and Nubian giraffes, for example, have dark spots with irregular edges. Others, such as the Transvaal giraffes, have spots with fingerlike projections. The reticulated giraffes have a more regular netlike pattern of dark patches divided by light lines.

In the wildlife park where Easter lived, the original giraffes were the Nubian and reticulated types. Because they interbreed, some of the giraffes in the park, like Easter, are a mixture of the two kinds. His lighter color is like that of the reticulated giraffes, but his spots have irregular edges like those of

Reticulated giraffe

Nubian giraffe

the Nubian giraffes. Giraffes in the wild also interbreed, creating many small variations in coloring.

Some scientists think that the spots help the giraffes to blend into a shadowy forest. Their body, too, acts as a camouflage. When a giraffe is standing at the edge of a forest, its long neck can look like just another tree trunk.

However, when the giraffe moves or stands in the open, its huge shape is hard to miss.

Although patterns are similar within a subspecies of giraffe, no two giraffes have exactly the same markings. Scientists who study giraffes use neck patterns like fingerprints to identify the individual animals.

13

Perhaps the most unusual feature of a giraffe is its 6-foot-long (1.8-meter-long) neck. Inside the neck is the windpipe, which conducts air from the nose and mouth to the lungs. The giraffe's lungs are larger in proportion to its body than those of other animals. The extra size is needed to pump air down the long neck. Without this extra power, the giraffe would breathe the same air in as it breathed out, and it would never get any fresh air.

14

The giraffe's 25-pound (11.4-kilogram) heart is also oversize in order to drive blood 8 feet (2.4 meters) upward to the head. Its blood pressure, which is two to three times that of a human, is higher than any other animal's.

As in the necks of other mammals, including humans, the giraffe's neck has only seven bones. These bones are huge and extremely heavy, and the neck muscles must be very strong to support them.

The head of a giraffe is topped by two blunt horns, which in males can be up to 9 inches (23 centimeters) long and 6 inches (15.4 centimeters) around. Female horns are thinner. Unlike the antlers of animals such as deer and elk, which are shed and regrown each year, these hair-covered horns are permanent.

At birth, the giraffe's horns are small knobs of cartilage. As they grow, the cartilage is gradually replaced by bone. Even after that, the horns continue to grow. Some giraffes also have a large, hair-covered bump on the forehead, which is called the *median horn.*

Male giraffes sometimes fight with their heads and necks in a ritual called *necking* or *head slamming.* The skull of a male giraffe can weigh up to 24 pounds (10.9 kilograms) and can be used like the end of a club in battle. One giraffe lowers his head, swinging it suddenly against the neck of his opponent. At the same time the other giraffe swings away and tries to return the blow. Each tries to jab his horns into the tender underside of the other's neck. Although these heavy blows hurt, they are not meant to wound the other animal. Fights among males are usually over the right to mate with a female.

At mating time, a male and female giraffe may rub heads and necks in what appears to be a show of affection.

Although male and female giraffes have a similar shape, the males, which are called *bulls,* are larger and more muscular. Their legs alone are over 6 feet (1.8 meters) long and their usual full-grown height is between 15 and 17 feet (4.6 and 5.2 meters). Giraffes are the tallest of all land animals, and the biggest one ever measured was 19 feet 3 inches (5.9 meters) tall!

An adult male giraffe can weigh 3,000 pounds (1,363.6 kilograms) or more. Although a giraffe does not reach full size until it is seven or eight, a male can mate when he is three to four years old.

In the wild, a male giraffe usually stays by himself and roams over a wide area. Females, on the other hand, stay together in pairs or small herds. A male may join a group of females when a female in the herd is ready to mate. He will stay with her for a few days, mate, and then leave. Giraffe herds are loosely organized, and animals come and go freely. Although herds sometimes number up to seventy, they usually have forty animals or less.

Female giraffes are called *cows.* They usually stand about 14 feet (4.3 meters) tall and can weigh as much as 2,500 pounds (1,136.4 kilograms). They are ready to mate when they are about three years old.

Female (front), male (rear)

After mating, a female giraffe is pregnant for about fifteen months before giving birth to a single baby. Occasionally, twins are born. At the wildlife park, several of the female giraffes were pregnant. One of them, June, looked as if she would have her baby soon. Each day, her belly seemed to get a little bit rounder. When her baby was born, it would join Easter as a youngster in the herd.

Baby giraffes are called *calves*. When they are born, they are 6 feet (1.8 meters) tall and weigh 150 pounds (68.2 kilograms). Like all baby animals, they grow rapidly in the first few months. At one point, Easter had grown 9 inches (23 centimeters) in just one week. By the time he became a year old, he would be about 10 feet (3 meters) tall.

Like other mammals, a giraffe mother feeds her baby milk. When the baby is hungry, it sucks the milk from one of the four teats on its mother's underside.

During Easter's first month, his only food was milk. If his own mother was not nearby, one of the other female giraffes in the herd that had milk for her own baby would allow him to nurse. In the wild and in the park, giraffe mothers often take turns "baby-sitting" the young giraffes in the herd. At the age of four months, even though Easter was almost independent, he still liked an occasional drink of milk from his mother.

Browsing giraffe in Nairobi National Park, Kenya

Like many of the animals of the African plains, such as zebras, gazelles, elands, and wildebeests, giraffes are plant eaters. Animals such as giraffes that eat leaves are said to browse.

At the park, the giraffes ate grass and hay as well as the special nutritional pellets that were part of the park diet for them. As the youngest in the herd, Easter was always the slowest and last to arrive at the feed bin, but each day he grew a little bigger and a little more sure of himself.

Giraffes will eat almost any kind of leaves, but in the wild their favorites are those of the whistling thorn acacia tree. The giraffe's body is particularly well adapted to this treetop diet. Its long neck allows it to browse far above the height that other plant-eating animals can reach. Also, a long, hairy upper lip and a thick mucous coating on the mouth and tongue prevent injury from the sharp acacia thorns.

To eat, a giraffe extends its 18-inch-long (46-centimeter-long) tongue and deftly plucks the leaf. It pulls the leaf into its mouth and bites it off with sharp front teeth. Then it chews the leaf with flat molar teeth in the back of the mouth.

Like domestic cattle, a giraffe chews a cud. After food is swallowed, it is regurgitated, or coughed up, and chewed again. This helps to break down tough plant fibers so that they can be more fully digested. Unlike your stomach, which is a single compartment, the giraffe's stomach is divided into four sections, and food travels through each during the process of digestion.

A full-grown bull giraffe has a huge appetite. He needs to eat a lot to provide energy for his enormous body. In the wild, he eats about 74 pounds (33.6 kilograms) of acacia leaves a day. Giraffes often roam over large areas to find enough food. At the wildlife park, they are fed a healthy variety of foods but they still try to eat whatever leaves they can reach. In the park, the trees are protected by fences so the giraffes do not destroy them by eating too many leaves.

In the wild, the nutritious leaves of the acacia trees are so moist that they contain almost all the water a giraffe needs. However, when necessary, a giraffe will go to a water hole to drink.

For a giraffe, bending over to drink or eat is difficult because its neck does not reach the ground unless the animal bends and spreads its long legs. This is an awkward position, and it is hard for the giraffe to change it quickly. When a giraffe lowers its head, blood in the neck rushes to the brain—it is as if the animal is standing upside down. A giraffe's blood vessels have special adaptations that block the blood and keep it from moving too quickly to the head. Thus, the giraffe does not get dizzy when it moves its head up and down.

As Easter got older, he spent more and more time away from his mother. Like the other giraffes, he ate or rested most of each day. During the day, the adult giraffes usually rested standing up, but Easter's legs sometimes got so tired that he lay down. When he got up again, he had to be careful to get his balance and keep his long, skinny

legs from getting tangled together.

To get up, a giraffe first throws its neck back. As the neck comes forward, the giraffe rises to its knees. Using its neck again, it extends its hind legs. In a third movement, it frees the forelegs and stands on all four feet. Giraffes lie down only when they feel completely safe.

Despite their gangly look, giraffes are surprisingly graceful runners and can gallop as fast as 35 miles (56.5 kilometers) an hour. When they run, the back legs swing forward together on the outside as the front legs push backward. Sometimes all four feet are in the air at the same time as the legs push off the ground.

Although giraffes can run fast in short bursts of speed, they tire easily. They prefer to walk, usually at a slow, ambling pace. When they are pacing, the legs on each side of the body move forward together so that the giraffe appears to rock from side to side. At a distance, a herd of pacing giraffes looks something like a fleet of large spotted ships sailing across a grassy sea.

31

Giraffes rarely attack people or other animals. They prefer to run from danger rather than fight. However, a female giraffe protecting a baby can be dangerous and will try to kick anyone who comes too near. In the wild, even lions are afraid of an angry mother giraffe. Her hooves are hard, and a well-placed kick could be a death blow. Instead, a lion prefers to attack when the young giraffe is untended. In the wild, young giraffes often become victims of lions and other meat-eating animals.

Occasionally, a lion will attack a full-grown giraffe if it can catch the giraffe when its head is down. Then the lion leaps on the giraffe's neck, and the giraffe is unable to defend itself.

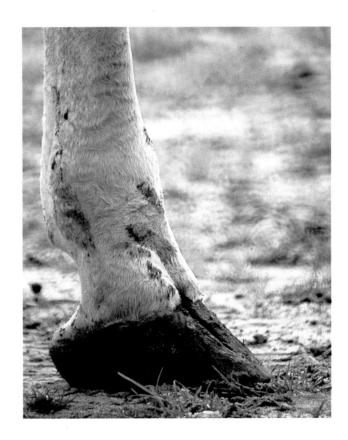

In the park, there was no need for Easter and the other giraffes to be on the lookout for lions, since the two animal species were kept in separate areas. Still, the giraffes were always alert and aware of new cars or people in their own enclosure.

In Africa, some people kill giraffes for their meat and hides. Giraffe tails are prized and used to make amulets and bracelets. Even though many giraffes in Africa live within areas where hunting is not allowed, they often wander out of the protected areas. Also, within national parks and reserves there are illegal hunters, or poachers.

On the open plains, it is extremely difficult for a hunter—either human or animal—to sneak up on a giraffe. The giraffe has excellent eyesight and a good sense of hearing. If it sees or hears anything unusual, the giraffe will stop what it is doing until it can decide whether or not there is danger nearby. Once a hunter has been discovered, it is impossible to make a surprise attack.

When one giraffe senses danger, it stands stiffly with its ears spread and tail switching. The other giraffes see this and are ready to follow if it is necessary to run.

Although giraffes are able to make noise and occasionally produce low moans or snorts when danger is near, they are usually silent.

At night on the African plains, the giraffes move into open areas. At the wildlife park, Easter and the other giraffes went into large barns. Usually, the females and young giraffes stayed together, and each male was kept in a separate stall. If it was rainy or cold, they stayed inside where it was warm and dry. On warm nights during the summer, the barn doors were left open and the giraffes were allowed to stay inside or move outside into a corral.

In the wild, giraffes are well adapted to the weather. Their thick skins keep them cool when it is hot, and warm during cold weather. Because winters in New Jersey are colder than the coldest nights in Africa, the giraffes in the park stay in the barns to keep warm.

37

Each day, the veterinarian who worked in the park checked on all the animals to see if any one was sick or needed treatment. Usually, he stopped to see the giraffes when they were still in the barns. The veterinarian was keeping a particularly close watch on June to see if she was getting ready to give birth. He knew it would be soon because he could see her belly bulge when the baby moved inside it.

In the morning, Easter was always eager to leave the barn and go out into the open area of the park. With the other giraffes, he waited for the keeper to unlock the gate. As soon as it opened, all the giraffes burst out and galloped across the grass in the cool air.

One morning as the giraffes left the barn, June lagged behind. When she walked, she looked as if she felt uncomfortable. All day, she stayed by herself, and when the other giraffes came near, she turned away. That night, when the giraffes went back into the barn, June stayed outside in the corral by herself.

The next morning, June was still standing in the corner of the corral, just where she had been the night before. But under her, on the ground, was a small newborn baby giraffe, its body still partly covered by the birth sac. Its soft fur was still wet and its big brown eyes blinked in the sunlight. It had been born just a few hours before. The vet and one of the keepers had stayed with June during the birth. If there had been any problem, they were there to help. They also made sure that no other people or animals disturbed June.

A mother giraffe gives birth standing up. The baby slips slowly out of the birth canal head and feet first, dropping about 6 feet (1.8 meters) to the ground. There it lies quietly as its mother licks it clean.

The female calf looked small compared to her 14-feet-tall (4.3-meter-tall) mother, although at 6 feet (1.8 meters) and 150 pounds (68.2 kilograms) she was huge in comparison to most other baby animals. This calf was healthy and hungry. Soon she would stand up to drink her mother's milk.

Like many other hooved animals, a newborn giraffe is able to stand from the first day of birth. It must be able to follow its mother and stay in the safety of the herd.

For a few days, June stayed alone with her new calf. Then they both joined the other giraffes in the herd. As the calf became older, she would be a companion for Easter.

Easter and the new baby giraffe will grow up in the comfort and security of the animal park. When they become adults, they will be able to mate and produce their own baby giraffes in safety. As long as they stay healthy, they can expect to live to be at least twenty-five years old.

Although most varieties of giraffes, including those that live in the wildlife park, are not threatened with extinction, their numbers have grown smaller in recent years. Much of the land where wild giraffes live has been converted to farms or grazing land for domestic cattle.

Today, zoos, parks, governments, and private organizations are helping to protect endangered animals, but as the African continent continues to be developed, areas for wildlife are growing smaller and smaller. It is important to preserve some portions for wild animals such as giraffes. For them, the African plains have always been home, and because they are so uniquely adapted to this land, there is nowhere else to go. The giraffe is a giant with an ancient heritage. The more we learn about these gentle animals, the better we will be at helping to ensure their future.

46

INDEX

Photographs are in **boldface**.